Surviving D-Day

Paul Challen

rosen publishing's
rosen central

New York

Published in 2016 by The Rosen Publishing Group, Inc.
29 East 21st Street, New York, NY 10010

Copyright © 2016 by The Rosen Publishing Group, Inc.

First Edition

Developed and produced for Rosen by BlueApple*Works* Inc.

Art Director: T.J. Choleva

Managing Editor for BlueApple*Works*: Melissa McClellan
Designer: Joshua Avramson
Photo Research: Jane Reid
Editor: Marcia Abramson

Library of Congress Cataloging-in-Publication Data

Challen, Paul C. (Paul Clarence), 1967-

Surviving D-Day/Paul Challen.—First edition.

    pages cm.—(Surviving disaster)

Includes bibliographical references and index.

ISBN 978-1-4994-3653-2 (library bound)—ISBN 978-1-4994-3655-6 (pbk.)—
ISBN 978-1-4994-3656-3 (6-pack)

1. World War, 1939-1945—Campaigns—France—Normandy—Juvenile literature. I. Title.

D756.5.N6C45 2016

940.54'21421—dc23

2015005634

Manufactured in the United States of America

Contents

Chapter 1
WWII in Europe 5

Chapter 2
June 6, 1944: D-Day 11

Chapter 3
The Midnight Wave 15

Chapter 4
Storming the Beaches 21

Chapter 5
Expanding the Foothold 37

Chapter 6
D-Day's Aftermath and Legacy 43

Glossary 46

For More Information 47

Index 48

Led by tanks, Germany's armored *panzer* divisions quickly rolled to early victories in World War II.

World War II, also called the Second World War, was fought during the years of 1939–1945. It was the largerst and most destructive global war the world has ever seen. **World War II** was also the deadliest military conflict in history. It is estimated that between 50 million and 85 million people died in the war.

The war started on September 1, 1939, when **Nazi** Germany attacked Poland. Great Britain and France, bound by a treaty with Poland, declared war on Germany in response. Although many nations took part, the two main sides in World War II were the **Axis powers**—Germany, Italy, and Japan—and the **Allied powers**—France, Great Britain, the United States, and the Soviet Union. Both alliances were joined in their efforts with several other countries.

Much of the initial fighting in World War II took place in Europe. The first major battles were fought in Poland, western Europe, and on vast stretches of the Soviet Union's territory. As the war progressed, other battles were fought in Africa and in the Mediterranean region.

The German military perfected the ability to strike quickly and with dealy effect. The leader of Germany, Adolf Hitler, and his generals employed a new kind of military tactics called the blitkrieg. It involved swift movement of moto-rized tank and panzer units, which was very effective in destroying and conquering large areas of territory quickly. The panzer units were supported from the air by squadrons of bomber planes, which provided massive air bombardments to weaken the enemy's defenses.

The blitzkrieg tactics proved to be surprisingly effective. Poland was overrun and surrendered in five weeks. Germany attacked in the west on May 10, 1940. Belgium and the Netherlands surrendered within the same month. Paris, the French capital, fell to the Germans on June 14, 1940. Great Britain, protected by the waters of **English Channel**, remained the last stronghold of the Allies. The Germans had to defeat Britain's Royal Air Force (RAF) in order to secure the channel for the invasion of the British Isles. When the German air force failed to win air superiority in 1940, Hitler postponed the invasion until the spring of 1941. Encouraged by swift victories in Western Europe, Nazi Germany invaded the Soviet Union in June 1941.

Following quick victories in the beginning of the Russian campaign, the German army suffered many defeats and setbacks. The German invasion of Great Britain was postponed indefinitely. Great Britain thus became the Allied fortress in the fight against Hitler's Germany.

USA Enters the Conflict

The United States was staying neutral under laws passed after World War I. President Franklin D. Roosevelt, though, believed that the Axis powers eventually would threaten the United States. He convinced Congress to pass the Lend-Lease Act, which allowed Americans to loan, lease, sell, or trade arms and food to countries that the president considered vital to national security. Under this law, the United States was able to send a massive amount of aid to Britain and the Soviet Union.

What many Americans did not want to send was troops. They believed that because the conflict was taking place far from their own country, it was not worth risking the lives of thousands of soldiers to join in. But that all changed on December 7, 1941. On that day, Japanese bomber planes attacked the United States Pacific Fleet at the naval base at Pearl Harbor, Hawaii. This attack came even though Japan and the U.S. were not at war with one another. It was designed to knock out American power in the South Pacific region.

The United States had no choice from that point onwards than to join the Allied forces against Germany, Japan, and Italy. Once the American military forces began taking part in the war, they had an immediate impact on land, in the air, and on the water.

Allied leaders Winston Churchill (left), Franklin Roosevelt (middle) and Josef Stalin (right) met in late 1943 and again in early 1945.

American military forces played important roles in victories against the Axis powers in North Africa and on the island of Sicily in the Mediterranean Sea. Indeed, with the contribution of the American troops, the Allies started winning important victories against their Axis enemies in both, European and Pacific theaters of World War II.

The Allies, led by the Big Three – U.S. President Franklin Roosevelt, British Prime Minister Winston Churchill, and Soviet leader Josef Stalin – decided that a major invasion of France was necessary as a decisive step toward winning the war. The Big Three began to plan for an invasion when they met in November 1943 in Tehran, in what is now Iran. Stalin wanted to set a specific date. His country was suffering terribly, and he knew the Germans would be stretched thin if they had to fight in both eastern and western Europe.

Roosevelt agreed but Churchill was reluctant. Britain had launched an amphibious attack on Dieppe, a French port, that ended in disaster in 1942. He eventually went along with the plan for an American-led invasion of northern France from England in the spring of 1944.

Crossing The English Channel

The English Channel is a 350-mile (563-km) stretch of water separating France and England. Until 1994, the only way to cross it was by boat. A popular ferry crossing took place between the English city of Dover and the French port of Calais. But since the completion of the "Chunnel" (or "channel tunnel"), it has been possible to drive across it. People on both sides of the channel had long said that it could never be overcome by military means. Until D-Day, no military force had crossed the channel successfully since William the Conqueror invaded England in 1066.

Troops trained hard in England for D-Day. They spent long hours with their tanks and planes, which they often nicknamed.

The Allies' plan involved a massive invasion – known as a "landing" – on a beach somewhere in northern France. The Allies called this "Operation Overlord" and considered several targets in this region. Immediately, it became clear that such an invasion would be very complicated, difficult to organize, and extremely challenging to carry out. First of all, the Allies had to decide where to land. **Normandy** was chosen because the Germans did not expect an attack there, but also because its beach terrain was similar to England's. This allowed troops in England to train and even test their tanks on similar ground.

U.S. troops had begun coming to England in late 1942 and trained all over the country. Vehicles, planes, ships, and weapons also were arriving. The Allies planned to land on French **beaches**, secure the harbors, and march inland. To lead the operation, the Allies named U.S. General Dwight D. Eisenhower as supreme commander in Europe in late 1943.

In advance of invasion, both bombing and reconnaissance flights were increased over northwest France. In addition, a long pipeline was built under the ocean to carry fuel from England to Normandy.

The Allies tried to keep these preparations as secret as possible, but they also knew that Germany had spies all over Britain. To confuse the Germans, a fake army with inflatable vehicles and wooden guns was set up across from the Calais region of France, north ofNormandy. It is closer to England, so the channel crossing would have been easier there. As a result, the Germans kept many troops and tanks in position to answer an invasion at Calais.

The Normandy coast, however, was not unprotected. The Germans were building what they called the **Atlantic Wall**, a line of heavily armed fortifications. By spring 1944, though, it was only half done. So the Germans filled the gaps by planting **mines**, laying barbed wire, and building sharp metal obstructions underwater to rip through any ships that tried to land on the beaches. The Allies knew they would have to break through these defenses.

Another important consideration regarding the planning of the invasion was the fact that the English Channel was notorious for having choppy, turbulent waters and stormy conditions, no matter what the time of year. The Allies needed to plan a time when a full moon would mean the tide was low enough to make obstacles the Germans had put in the water visible, and enough moonlight to make nighttime operations possible. This meant that there were only a few days each month when the invasion could take place.

Despite these huge challenges, the Allies proceeded with the invasion on a massive scale. Indeed, the D-Day invasion was – and is to this day – the biggest invasion by water that has ever taken place. The Normandy landings, known by the code name "D-Day," took place on June 6, 1944. This was actually one day later than planned, because the weather of June 5 was simply too poor for the landing ever to have a hope of being successful.

An estimated 160,000 Allied men took part on the day of the invasion, using almost 6,000 boats to do the job. Almost 5,000 of these were assault and **landing craft**, attacking the enemy and bringing men, weapons, and supplies onto the beach. Nearly 300 were minesweepers designed to explode mines harmlessly before they could destroy the Allied seaborne craft, and another almost 300 were escort vessels that would fire at the enemy while the Allies carried out operations.

Allied troops waited tensely, some for days, aboard ships in Southampton and other English ports.

Paratroopers waited to be dropped over Normandy, knowing that making a night jump was very risky.

Chapter 3
The Midnight Wave

Before naval forces could land on the beaches at Normandy, the Allies needed to weaken the German defenses. The D-Day plan included provisions for airborne assaults and air and naval bombing during the night of the landings in preparations for the main naval assault. The Allies planned for this "midnight wave" to be the first part of their successful invasion, as it would start to attack German soldiers and destroy their fortifications on the beach.

To help the Allied forces operate at night and at dawn, more than 3,200 reconnaissance flights had been flown over the Normandy beaches. Starting in April 1944, the planes swooped close to the ground to snap detailed photos of the terrain and the fortifications. The photos were used to make maps to help the ground forces reach their targets. In the sea, minesweepers went to work on the night of June 5 to help clear the way for the invasion fleet.

Around midnight on June 6, about 1,200 planes took off, carrying three divisions of paratroopers to make the dangerous drop behind enemy lines. Before dawn, waves of bombers began their runs to attack targets on the beaches.

Bombing of Normandy

American bombers played a massive role in attacking the German defenses so that targets such as bridges and villages could be captured more effectively by troops on the ground.

The Allies had been working to cripple German air power in order to have a successful invasion. By spring 1944, many German planes had been shot down in battles with Allied bombers and their escorts, and Allied bombs had destroyed many German airplane factories. This basically cleared the skies for the D-Day invasion.

During the assault, the American 8th and 9th Air Force attacked the Atlantic Wall, communications stations, and other strategic targets. They were supported by British and other Allied air units. Some of the squadrons protected the ships traveling from England to Normandy, while others attacked on the beaches.

Thirty-three of the 171 Allied squadrons went sent to attack other areas to keep the Germans confused about whether Normandy was the real invasion or a diversion. Some planes even dropped hundreds of dummy paratroopers at four different locations to make the Germans think that there was more than one area of invasion.

The Allies painted their planes with wide black-and-white stripes to avoid confusion during D-Day. Allied gunners were told to shoot at anything that didn't have stripes!

The weather, though, still was not cooperating. Cloudy skies and strong winds prevented some planes from completing their attack missions, especially at Omaha Beach, where bombers overshot their targets by several miles. The air assault on Utah Beach was much more successful in destroying German fortifications.

At 5:45 AM, a fierce naval bombardment was added to the air attack. Five battleships, sixty-five destroyers, and dozens of other ships began pounding the beach defenses.

The Airborne Assault

American planes also served to drop thousands of paratroopers to help secure the areas some distance behind the beaches in the enemy territory. The paratroopers, all volunteers, trained for two years for this moment. They carried heavy packs of equipment because they could not be sure where they would land or how soon they would find other Allied soldiers. Their goal was to take control of bridges, roads, railroad crossings, hills and other strategic points, which would make it easier for troops to move inland from the beaches.

After midnight on June 6, Allied paratroopers began parachuting from planes and gliders into the countryside

Survivor Account

Arthur Hopper was a glider pilot who took part in the D-Day invasions as part of the U.S. Army Air Forces. He trained in both the United States and England to get ready to play his part. On D-Day, he carried four paratroopers, radio equipment, and a jeep to his target in the early hours before the beach invasion. During the landing, he had been under fire from German guns as well. Although he did take part in ground fighting, Hopper knew that his main task was to keep on flying. "As glider pilots was it our objective to get troops and or equipment on the ground," he recalled. "And then get back to the main sea landing area as soon as possible, to perhaps go on another airborne effort."

Glider planes often broke up when they landed.
Troops had to regroup quickly and get moving.

around the beaches. West of Utah Beach, the American 82nd and 101st Airborne Divisions had one of the toughest jobs of D-Day. They were assigned to take control of narrow causeways through low-lying areas that the Germans had flooded as part of their defenses. Amid dense clouds and strong wind, pilots often missed the planned drop zones. Some paratroopers were mowed down when they landed right on top of German forces. Others drowned in the flooded areas; still others died when parachutes failed. Planes that were shot down out of the sky often crashed and burned with men inside

But despite the heavy loses, airborne attacks and support – led by the efforts of the American paratroopers – were absolutely crucial to Allied success on D-Day and the weeks that followed.

Ships unloaded men, tanks, trucks, and supplies at low tide on Omaha Beach. Stationary blimps called barrage balloons were positioned to help deter air attacks.

Chapter 4

Storming the Beaches

The D-Day invasion plan was for the Allies to capture a fifty-mile section of the coastline. They divided this area into five sections as part of their planning, and had a strategy for capturing all of them. The Allies called these the Utah, Omaha, Gold, Juno, and Sword Beaches.

About 73,000 U.S. troops landed at Utah and Omaha Beach, 62,000 British troops at Sword and Gold, and 21,000 Canadians at Juno. The plan was for the Americans to march to the port of Cherbourg with the British and Canadians protecting them.

The first Allied soldiers landed at 6:30 AM on Omaha Beach. Many jumped off their transports into a hail of machine gun fire. The situation was different at each beach, depending on how much damage the air and sea bombardment had done there. Many beaches had high cliffs looking over them. The invading Allies needed to come up the beach from the water and then scale those cliffs, while the Germans were able to stand on top and fire down at them. As the Allies tried to wade through the water and onto drier land, German bullets flew all around them. Unfortunately for many of the brave men that stormed the beaches in the first wave of the invasion, there were many casualties.

Utah Beach

Utah Beach was the westernmost of D-Day's five targeted beaches to be reached by the Allied forces. Surprisingly, the forces of nature that the Allies had been concerned about when planning the invasions played a role in helping them storm Utah Beach successfully. That's because as the first troops approached the shore around 6 AM, they found their boats drifting off course owing to the strong English Channel currents. In fact, these troops ended up more than a mile to the south of where they had intended to come ashore. But this ended up being fortunate because it put them in a spot that was defended by just one German position, and not two as would have been the case at the intended target. What's more, the lone German position had earlier been hit hard by Allied bombers. Unlike neighboring Omaha Beach, the preliminary aerial bombardment was highly effective at Utah.

Once the first troops had landed on Utah Beach, they were joined by **amphibious tanks** and explosives experts. Their job was to begin clearing the beach, removing dangerous barriers and mines the Germans had placed there. They also smashed the sea wall near the beach with explosives, allowing men and tanks to come ashore more easily.

Communication was difficult, so U.S. soldiers put out an American flag to show Allied gunners that they had taken a key cliff west of Omaha Beach.

By 9 o'clock, troops ready to engage the Germans in combat began to move inland. They headed quickly for Cherbourg, a city north of Juno Beach. The Allies need to secure Cherbourg quickly so they could use its large port facilities.

As the enemy had flooded the fields behind the beach, it was hard going for many of the troops who were traveling on foot but wanted to avoid the lone road going inland.

Survivor Account

Captain Tallie J. Crocker led a team of men onto Utah Beach on D-Day. He remembers crossing the English Channel as a time of great activity. "There were ships as far as the eye could see," Captain Crocker recalled. "It was a sight to behold." Captain Crocker took his men through German fire and onto the beach, and credits the training they had done prior to the invasion as a big part of their successful landing. "None of my men had been killed or seriously wounded when we arrived on the beach," he said. "Moving inland on the causeway it was a sudden shock to us to see that others had not been so lucky. This was where we found the first American and German dead."

As the Allied tanks and troops moved steadily away from the beach, they began facing the Germans, who used anti-tank guns and rifles to try to repel them. This did not stop the Allies from capturing much of the area quickly, though Cherbourg held out until June 26.

The invasion of Utah Beach had not gone exactly as planned because of the one-mile "drift" of the landing troops crossing the English Channel, but the main area had been captured. As well, 21,000 troops Allied had come ashore and could begin moving on to new targets. Sadly, just under 200 of them had been killed in the fighting to take Utah Beach and the area around it.

Omaha Beach

The landing on Omaha Beach did not go as smoothly for the Allies as their efforts on Utah Beach. The same strong currents that benefitted the Utah invaders caused problems with the Omaha force. Because many of the troops had been forced farther east than they had expected, the American bomber planes had been wary of hitting the area. This meant that many of the German targets had not been attacked prior to the landing, making them harder to overcome.

As well, the troops found their landing craft stuck on sandbars as they neared the shore, and they had to wade through neck-deep water and enemy bullets to get onto the beach. Also because of the rough water, thirty-two Allied amphibious tanks were dropped from their carrier ships almost three miles from shore and struggled to make it to the beach. Unfortunately, thirty-three crew members drowned as twenty-seven of the tanks flooded and sank.

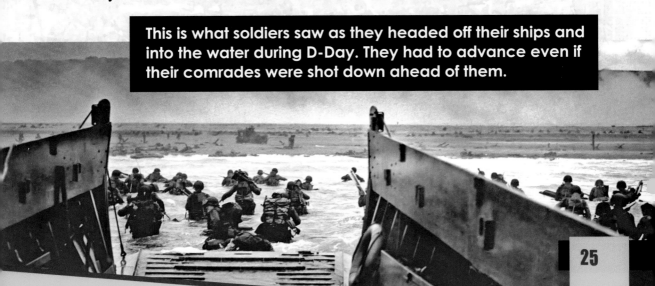

This is what soldiers saw as they headed off their ships and into the water during D-Day. They had to advance even if their comrades were shot down ahead of them.

By the end of June 9, the Allies could unload men and supplies safely on Omaha Beach.

Finally, the German force awaiting the Allies at Omaha was much bigger than the Allies had anticipated. In fact, of the five D-Day beaches, this was the one with the most defenses, again making it harder to invade and clear of obstacles. Although the first troops had come onto the shore early in the morning, just a few hours after that the invasion leaders decided to stop vehicles from trying to land for a short time – only to resume landings when destroyer ships arrived to support them.

Despite these problems, the Allies fought hard to claim Omaha Beach. A few hours later, 600 troops had moved up the beach and by noon some of the beach had been cleared of the enemy. It took almost four full days to completely secure Omaha Beach, at a cost of about 2,000 Allied men – but by June 9, it had been secured. As well, the Allies were able to secure Pointe du Hoc, an area with a dangerous German gun battery. This was a key area because it contained high ground and connected the Utah and Omaha Beaches

Survivor Account

Landings on all five Normandy beaches were made difficult by choppy conditions on the English Channel. Many men, even those who were experienced at crossing large bodies of water in preparation for battle, found seasickness a big problem. Just consider what Mike McKinney, who was part of one of the first waves of troops to arrive on Omaha, had to say about the crossing. "On all the occasions that I had been on a landing craft, if it was the (United) States, Tunisia, or Sicily, I never once got sick," he recalled. "This time in the English Channel, I did get sick." McKinney managed to regain his composure and jumped out of his boat with about 80 pounds (36 kg) of equipment on his back, ready to do battle on Omaha Beach.

Gold Beach

The Germans also had strong defenses on the third of the planned Normandy invasion points, the 5-mile (8-km) long Gold Beach. Strategically, this was an important point as it lay in the middle of the five beaches. Most dangerously for the Allies, there were four large guns atop the beach that the enemy could use to blast down at them as they tried to come ashore. The Allied solution was to use cruiser ships to fire at the gun battery, and this proved to be successful. Just after 6 AM, two cruisers knocked out three of the four guns with hits to the battery. The Germans continued to use the fourth one, but they were only able to keep using it until the next day before surrendering their former strongpoint.

Survivor Account

Englishman Stanley Cox was aboard one of the first tanks to reach Gold Beach. Almost sixty years later, doctors were amazed to find that he had not completely left the invasion behind him. As one of the first Allies to liberate a French town, Cox had been wounded in an arm, a leg, and in his buttocks, and spent nine months in the hospital recovering from his injuries. Many decades later, planning a visit to Normandy for a reunion, he fell and broke his hip. When in the hospital, it was discovered that he still had quite a bit of shrapnel in him from his wounds!

Gold Beach was also the location of part of what was known as the **Mulberry Harbor**. This was an amazing construction of two human-made harbors that were towed across the Channel and assembled off the Normandy beaches. Joining Omaha and Gold Beaches, it was made up of about six miles of steel roadways that could allow up to 7,000 tons of vehicles, troops, and equipment per day. The whole thing floated on a system of steel and concrete supports – and it was protected by a wall of sunken ships, barriers, and floating breakwaters. Today, many people consider the Mulberry Harbor one of the most impressive feats of construction built during World War II.

As was the case on the other beaches, troops trying to land on Gold Beach found it difficult going because of the weather. Allied bombers had tried to hit another German target with a powerful gun as well as a sea wall protecting the beach, but had not been very effective.

Mulberry Harbor was a British idea that really worked. The Allies brought their own port so they did not need to capture one immediately.

By late afternoon on June 7, the German fortifications had been knocked out on Gold Beach.

Landing troops faced a lot of fire on the east side of the beach until well into the afternoon. The Allied troops were able to overcome this, though, and soon started capturing many of the houses that the German troops had taken over and were using as shelter as they fought.

Gradually, the Allies moved inland and captured a small port at the town of Port-en-Bessin, and, eventually, after much fighting, the important town of Bayeux. When Gold Beach was finally captured, the Allies estimated they had lost 1,000 men in the fighting.

Juno Beach

The Allies aimed to begin the invasion of the fourth beach, Juno, just before 5 AM. They planned this attack to happen at the same time as low tide, which would allow them to come ashore more easily. However, the attack was delayed about three hours, again because of rough water, and the landing troops actually arrived too early to be supported by heavy guns as had been the plan. German mines destroyed many Allied landing crafts, and German fire hit the troops hard when they came onto the beach. Also, the Allies' bombing efforts had not been very successful, meaning that many of the German defensive positions were intact as the Allies invaded.

As the Allies stormed onto Juno Beach they looked for ways to move inland. One of the D-Day invasion's most unusual maneuvers happened when Allied soldiers took a huge tank and used it to fill a crater – then covered the tank with wood and other material to make a temporary crossing point for troops and equipment. Amazingly, this tank stayed on the beach for almost thirty more years!

The Germans had many well-defended points in the towns near Juno Beach, and the Allies fought fierce battles in and around the towns' captured houses. As well, both sides fought hard in the battle over an airfield in the area, which would be an important area for planes to take off and land. It took about one month for this airfield to be won by the Allies. Eventually the Germans were overcome, but an estimated 1,000 men lost their lives at and around Juno Beach.

However, this was a key victory for the Allies. Not only had another important German position been captured, but more importantly, the joining of the Juno and Gold Beaches meant that now the Allies had control of a large area off the Normandy coast, measuring 12 miles (19 km) wide and 7 miles (11 km) deep.

Survivor Account

Before the D-Day invasions could take place, many thousands of men had to go through extensive training. For American soldiers, this took place both at home and in England. One veteran of the invasion, Jack Mills, recalled what the training was like at Camp Picket, Virginia. "We started with our 'Amphibious Training,'" he said. "We didn't know what it was or what it meant until later, but we were training for the D-Day landing in Normandy. This is when they took us out from the beach to an old ship anchored offshore outside the breakers in the rough water and we had to climb a rope ladder. It really wasn't a ladder but a large rope net-like thing slung over the side of the ship." It was by learning to climb this makeshift equipment that Mills and his fellow trainees would begin to prepare for D-Day.

Canadian forces came ashore in waves at Juno Beach. By the end of June 6 they had fought their way farther inland than any other group.

Sword Beach

The fifth of the D-Day landing areas was Sword Beach – the easternmost of the five beaches. It was close to the city of Caen, which was an important target for the Allies to attack – and the Germans to defend – because many of the roads of Normandy crossed through there.

The first troops landed on Sword Beach just before 7:30 AM and by 8 AM the force of British commandos had taken control of the beach. Although the Allied efforts seemed easy to this point, that was about to change as the Germans launched a counterattack. Allied troops on Sword Beach

Survivor Account

As well-planned and, finally, successful as the D-Day invasions were, it was impossible to carry out military actions with that many men, and so much equipment, without error. A soldier named Henry Weir recalled one terrible incident that, luckily, did not have a bad ending. "A P-51 Mustang [an American plane] came in flying low over the beach," Weir said. "The pilot must have been really confused, because he strafed the soldiers on the beach with his machine guns. Up to this day I can still not understand how the pilot mistook us for German soldiers." Happily, Weir said that this mistake was not fatal: "I did not see any casualties as a result of his dumb mistake."

British forces landed easily but then had to fight off a counterattack at Sword Beach.

had planned to meet up with their counterparts from Juno, but this did not happen. A large force of German panzer tanks and troops hit back, and about 12 hours after the Allies had taken control it looked as if the Germans might retake the beach. But Allied planes were able to bomb the Panzer division and, supported by tanks, repelled the German counterattack.

At the end of June 6, almost 30,000 men had come ashore on Sword Beach, and only 630 casualties had been suffered by the Allies. It still took the Allies seven weeks to liberate the town of Caen, but they finally managed to take control of this major transportation zone.

Securing the beaches allowed many more Allied troops to land. By the end of June, the Allies controlled Normandy.

Chapter 5
Expanding the Foothold

Once the Allies had captured all five of the D-Day beaches, they had to continue their operations by connecting, or "linking" them all in a continuous line about 60 miles (97 km) long and 15 miles (24 km) deep along the Normandy coast. This was a difficult challenge, but it was an absolutely crucial part of the Allies' strategy. If this linking could not succeed, all of the effort spent on the invasion of the five beaches would go to waste.

The key to these linking operations was to first secure the Allied military position on the beaches, known as bridgeheads. Once victory had been assured on Utah, Omaha, Gold, Juno and Sword Beaches, they needed to be connected by taking over all the territory between them. In fact, only Juno and Gold beaches were connected on June 6, the first day of the invasion. Additionally, the Allies did not succeed right away in going as far inland to retake several towns as they had planned.

The German resistance in the small towns just inland from the Normandy coast was fierce. They realized that the Allies were planning to use this part of Northern France as a starting point for liberating Western Europe.

German troops wanted to defend it at all costs. There was a lot of very close fighting, as both the Allies and the Germans took over homes and buildings in these towns, exchanging gunfire from these positions. Many small bridges became places were a lot of fighting took place as well. The Allies were determined to take over the bridges because this would allow them to move on to the territory that lay beyond them.

Another big obstacle was the fact that, in the early part of the D-Day invasions, the Allies had not managed to take control of a port, which would allow them to bring in supplies and men more easily.

Survivor Account

Bill Rugh was a U.S. Navy gunloader on a large ship that took part in the D-Day invasion. He grew up in a large family of sixteen in a small town in Pennsylvania and signed up for the war effort when he was eighteen. Although the United States entered the war in 1941 and fought with the Allies until 1945, Bill – like many Americans – never thought the war would last that long. "We were all quite shaken when the Japanese attacked Pearl Harbor," he said. "I remembering my Dad saying, 'In three months' time we'll defeat them.' As we know it didn't happen like that, it was a long, hard-fought war with the loss of life heavy on all sides."

Many U.S. troops awaited D-Day in LCT-class ships. LCT stands for "landing craft tank.

Ports in France quickly became jammed with Allied military supplies as they were liberated.

They had built artificial harbors along the coast to help with this, but needed a true port with all of its facilities for loading and unloading to truly be effective. The Allied plan called for a capture of the port of Cherbourg, but they were not able to take control of it immediately.

The Allies continued to press on, battling the Germans at key strategic points all along Normandy. The fighting was very fierce, with many casualties on both sides. Some of the German army's leaders had begun to disagree with the military strategies put forth by Hitler, and disorganization certainly helped the Allies' efforts.

Finally, by June 12, six days after the invasion, the Allies had successfully linked all five bridgeheads. By June 26, Cherbourg had been taken. These victories meant that they now had a strong position along the Atlantic from which to move on into the rest of Western Europe. Near the start of the war, Adolf Hitler had ordered his troops to build a strong, "Atlantic Wall" from Norway in the north and Spain in the south, well defended by men and weapons. With the linking of the Normandy beaches, the Atlantic Wall had truly been smashed.

D-Day's Only Woman Invader

While many thousands of men took part in the D-Day invasion, only one woman did: the famous American reporter Martha Gellhorn. This legendary war correspondent was born in St. Louis in 1908. As a woman she could not get permission to join the invasion as a member of the press, but she made history when she hid in a hospital ship to cross the Channel, and then pretended to be a stretcher bearer when the ship landed. Gellhorn covered many of World War II's battles and later remembered: "I followed the war wherever I could reach it." Gellhorn was married for a time to the famous writer Ernest Hemingway. She died in 1989.

Allied forces raised the flags of Britain, France, and the United States as they liberated France.

Chapter 6
D-Day's Aftermath and Legacy

The D-Day invasions were very costly in terms of men. Historians generally place the loss of life among the Allies at about 10,000 on just the first two days of the invasion. Somewhere between 4,000 and 9,000 Germans also died. During the entire Normandy campaign, more than 400,000 soldiers are estimated to have died. Many people find it hard to imagine that the number of troops equal to a large city could have been lost in such a short time, but unfortunately this is true.

But the victory over the Germans was tremendously important to the overall Allied strategy in attempting to win the war. Once the German defenses had been broken in Northern France, it was possible for the Allies to move into the rest of France and then Europe to defeat the German positions there, and to liberate people there from the Nazis who had taken their towns and cities. For example, on August 25, Allied forces took back Paris, the largest city in France and the national capital. This was very important for the French people and for other Europeans who were still opposing the Nazis.

The Soviets had been fighting fiercely since 1941 on the Eastern Front. They launched a major offensive in early 1945 to push back the Nazis. The Germans had committed many troops to the Eastern Front, but with their defeat in the western part of the continent become final, it was hard for them to hold on in the east as well.

Adolf Hitler died on April 30, 1945. On May 7, 1945, the Germans surrendered. Within two days, Germans on the Eastern Front also surrendered.

Although most World War II historians do not claim that D-Day "won the war" for the Allies, they do agree that the courageous and well-planned invasion of June 6, 1944, certainly played a very important part in the outcome.

Today, it is possible for visitors to Normandy to visit the sites of the D-Day invasion. These are good reminders of the bravery and heroism of the Allied war efforts, but also reminders of how terrible war can be when it comes to loss of life and injuries.

Many streets are named after Allied battle units who fought there, and there are historical plaques, museums, and markers all across the region. There is a large American cemetery in the town of Colleville-sur-Mer comme-morating the U.S. soldiers who died in the invasion. In the town of Bayeux, there is also a large British war cemetery, and there are Polish and Canadian cemeteries as well.

A total of 9,387 American soldiers are burried in Colleville-sur-Mer. The cemetery is located on a bluff overlooking the Omaha Beach.

Glossary

Allied powers The combined forces of the United Kingdom, the United States, Canada, the Soviet Union, and France that opposed the Axis powers in the global conflict in World War II.

amphibious tanks Military vehicles that are capable of traveling both on land and in the water.

Atlantic Wall The system of defenses set up by Germany in the Atlantic Ocean during the first part of World War II.

Axis powers The combined forces of Germany, Italy, and Japan that formed one side of World War II in opposition to the Allies

beaches The key invasion points of the D-Day invasion. The five D-Day beaches were Utah, Omaha, Juno, Gold and Sword Beaches.

English Channel The body of water separating France and England. It is about 350 miles long.

landing craft Boats that were used by the Allies to come ashore onto the D-Day beaches.

mines Explosive devices that were used extensively on the D-Day beaches and in the English Channel.

Mulberry Harbor A human-made system of steel and concrete that allowed the Allies to connect the Gold and Omaha Beaches after the initial D-Day invasions.

Nazi Nazi followers of Adolf Hitler and the ruling National Socialist Party in Germany; often the plural form is used to refer to the German government and people during World War II.

Normandy The region of Northern France that was the location for the D-Day invasions.

panzer A form of military tank that was widely and effectively used by German forces to defend against the Allies in the D-Day invasion, and throughout World War II.

paratroopers Allied soldiers who jumped from planes or gliders during the invasion of the Normandy beaches.

World War II The massive global conflict that involved more than 30 countries and was waged between 1939 and 1945.

For More Information

Books

Adams, Simon. *DK Eyewitness Books: World War II.*
New York, NY: DK Books, Reprint edition 2014.

Atkinson, Rick. *D-Day: The Invasion of Normandy, 1944.*
New York, NY: Henry Holt and Co., 2014.

Biskup, Agnieszka. *D-Day: June 6, 1944.*
Portsmouth, NH: Heinemann, 2014.

Websites

Because of the changing nature of Internet links, Rosen Publishing has developed an online list of websites related to the subject of this book. This site is updated regularly. Please use this link to access this list:

http://www.rosenlinks.com/SD/D-Day

Index

A

Africa, 5, 8
Airborne Divisions, 19
Allied powers, 5
amphibious tanks, 22, 25
anti-tank guns, 24
Atlantic Wall, 12, 16, 41
Axis powers, 5, 7, 8

B

Bayeux, 30, 44
Belgium, 6
blitzkrieg, 6
bomber planes, 6, 7, 25
bombers, 15, 16, 17, 22, 29
bridgeheads, 37, 41
Britain's Royal Air Force
  (RAF), 6

C

Caen, 34, 35
Cherbourg, 21, 23, 24, 40, 41
Churchill, Winston, 8, 9
coastline, 21
Colleville-sur-Mer, 44, 45
Cox, Stanley, 28
Crocker, Tallie J., 24

D

destroyers, 17
Dieppe, 9

E

Eastern Front, 44
Eisenhower, Dwight D., 11
English Channel, 6, 9, 12, 22,
  24, 27
Europe, 3, 5, 6, 7, 9, 11, 37,
  41, 43

F

France, 5, 9, 11, 12, 37, 40,
  42, 43

G

Gellhorn, Martha, 41
Germany, 4, 5, 6, 7, 12
Gold Beach, 21, 28, 29, 30,
  32, 37
Great Britain, 5, 6, 7, 9, 12, 42

H

Hitler, Adolf, 6, 41, 44
Hopper, Arthur, 18

I

Italy, 5, 7

J

Japan, 5, 7
Juno Beach, 21, 23, 31, 32, 33,
  35, 37

L

landing, 11, 13, 18, 24, 25, 27,
  31, 32, 34, 39

M

McKinney, Mike, 27
Mills, Jack, 32
mines, 12, 13, 22, 31
minesweepers, 13, 15
Mulberry Harbor, 29

N

Nazi(s), 5, 6, 43, 44
Netherlands, 6
Normandy, 11, 12, 13, 14, 15,
  16, 27, 28, 29, 32, 34, 36, 37,
  40, 41, 43, 44

O

Omaha Beach, 17, 20, 21, 22,
  23, 25, 26, 27, 29, 37, 45
Operation Overlord, 11

P

panzer tanks, 35
panzer units, 6
paratroopers, 14, 15, 16,
  18, 19
Paris, 6, 43
Pearl Harbor, 7, 38
Poland, 5, 6

R

reconnaissance flights, 11, 15
Roosevelt, Franklin D., 7, 8, 9
Rugh, Bill, 38

S

Soviets, 44
Soviet Union, 5, 6, 7
Stalin, Josef, 8, 9
Sword Beach, 21, 34, 35, 37

U

United States, 2, 5, 7, 38, 42
Utah Beach, 17, 19, 21, 22, 24,
  25, 27, 37

W

Weir, Henry, 34
Western Europe, 6, 37, 41